W9-ASU-635

HEADLINE ISSUES

Animals Under Threat

Angela Royston

Heinemann Library
Chicago, Illinois

H **www.heinemannraintree.com**
Visit our website to find out
more information about
Heinemann-Raintree books.

To order:

☎ Phone 888-454-2279

💻 Visit www.heinemannraintree.com
to browse our catalog and order online.

© 2009 Heinemann Library
an imprint of Capstone Global Library, LLC
Chicago, Illinois

All rights reserved. No part of this publication may be
reproduced or transmitted in any form or by any means,
electronic or mechanical, including photocopying,
recording, taping, or any information storage and
retrieval system, without permission in writing from the
publisher.

Edited by Sarah Eason and Leon Gray
Designed by Calcium and Geoff Ward
Original illustrations © Capstone Global Library,
 LLC 2009
Illustrated by Geoff Ward
Picture research by Maria Joannou
Originated by Heinemann Library
Printed and bound in China by CTPS

13 12 11 10 09
10 9 8 7 6 5 4 3 2 1

Library of Congress Cataloging-in-Publication Data
Royston, Angela.
 Animals under threat / Angela Royston.
  p. cm. -- (Headline issues)
 Includes bibliographical references and index.
 ISBN 978-1-4329-2404-1 (hc) -- ISBN 978-1-4329-2415-7
(pb)
 1. Endangered species--Juvenile literature. 2. Wildlife
conservation--Juvenile literature. I. Title.
 QL83.R687 2008
 591.68--dc22
                    2008049508

Acknowledgments
The author and publishers are grateful to the following
for permission to reproduce copyright material:
Alamy Images: Rick & Nora Bowers 5t; Corbis: Roman
Poderni/R.P.G. 24b, Keren Su 11b; Digital Vision: Joel
Simon 16b; Dreamstime: Debra Law 30–31, Miao 10,
Peter Pomorski 26–27, Tomas Suchanek 4; FLPA: Fred
Bavendam/Minden Pictures 15t, Katherine Feng/Globio/
Minden Pictures 28b, Frans Lanting 9t, Yva Momatiuk/
John Eastcott/Minden Pictures 19l, Gordon Roberts
26b; Fotolia: Shock 28–29; Getty Images: The Image
Bank/Doug Allan 17, Minden Pictures/Zhinong Xi 23b;
Istockphoto: 7t, 15bg, 15b, Paul Loewen 18, 18–19, Karen
Locke 12–13, Sean Locke 13, Willie Manalo 8–9, Joerg
Reimann 27b, Scott Slattery 8–9; Photolibrary: Nordic
Photos/Inger Helene Boasson 12b; Rex Features: John
Cunningham 25b; Science Photo Library: Tony Camacho
7b; Shutterstock: 17, Brett Atkins 25, Sandy Buckley 12,
Steve Byland 9b, Mike Flippo 3, Andreas Gradin 19r,
Gueorgui Ianakiev 29, Arnold John Labrentz 7, Langdu
11, Nik Niklz 32, Tyler Olson 21t, Maxim S Pometun 21b,
Jose AS Reyes 6, Ian Scott 14, Kristian Sekulic 16, Helen
Shorey 22–23, 23t, Daniel W. Slocum 5b, Albert H. Teich
24, Steve Weaver 20, Peter Wey 1, 22–23.

Cover photograph reproduced with permission of
Istockphoto/Neal McClimon.

Every effort has been made to contact copyright holders
of any material reproduced in this book. Any omissions
will be rectified in subsequent printings if notice is given
to the publisher.

All the Internet addresses (URLs) given in this book
were valid at the time of going to press. However, due to
the dynamic nature of the Internet, some addresses may
have changed, or sites may have changed or ceased to
exist since publication. While the author and Publishers
regret any inconvenience this may cause readers, no
responsibility for any such changes can be accepted by
either the author or the Publishers.

Contents

Some words are printed in bold, **like this**. You can find out what they mean by looking in the glossary on page 30.

People Threaten Animals

PEOPLE HARM ANIMALS when they damage or destroy their **habitats**. Habitats are the places where the animals live. The destruction of habitats is killing many kinds of living creatures. Each kind of living thing is a different **species**. Some species are now so rare that they may die out altogether. When that happens, they will be **extinct**.

Destroying habitats

People destroy habitats when they build new towns, roads, and airports. They also destroy habitats when they change wild land into farmland. Dumping trash pollutes and damages habitats. Many wild animals can only live in a particular habitat. When this habitat is destroyed or damaged, the animals have to find a new home. If there is no similar habitat nearby, the animals may die.

Breaking food chains

When one species in a habitat becomes extinct, it affects many other animals that live in the same habitat. This is because each species relies on other species for food. Some animals eat other animals, which in turn may eat plants. The feeding relationships among different living things are collectively known as a food chain. If one animal is threatened or disappears from the food chain, all the other animals will be threatened.

For example, sea birds feed on fish. However, some people in Chile have been catching so many fish, there are not enough left for the sea birds to eat. This is called **overfishing**. Not only are there now fewer sea birds in Chile, but there are fewer fish to eat for the people who live there.

FACT!

◆ Over the past 35 years, one quarter of Earth's land animals have been wiped out by climate change or human activities.

ON THE SPOT
California

Pacific pocket mice live only on **scrubland** in southern California. The scrubland is by the coast, and there is now very little of it left. The rest has been changed into farms and towns. Pacific pocket mice have become extremely rare because they have lost almost all of their habitat.

The building of new houses and farms threatens the Pacific pocket mouse.

Sumatran tigers are so rare, there will soon be none left in the wild. Tigers will survive only in zoos and wildlife parks.

Destroyed by Fire and Felling

PEOPLE ARE DESTROYING huge areas of **rain forest** around the world. Many different plant **species** grow in these thick, damp forests. Destroying the plants destroys the **habitats** of millions of animals.

Ecologists are people who study living things and their habitats. They are alarmed because they think that up to 50,000 species are being wiped out every year.

Cutting down trees

Mahogany and teak both grow in rain forests. The wood from these trees is extremely valuable. As a result, **logging** companies cut down the trees. As they fall, the trees damage all the plants around them. Logging companies also fell the trees to make space for roads. Buying something made of mahogany or teak could be helping to destroy the rain forest.

Destroying rain forest

Companies and farmers burn large areas of rain forest. They clear the land to grow **crops**. Some companies plant palm trees. Farmers then harvest oil from the trees and use it as a fuel.

Poor soil

Some farmers plant grass in the cleared areas of rain forest. They need it to feed livestock such as cows. However, the rain forest soil is poor, so the crops and grass only grow well for a few years. Companies and farmers move on and clear more rain forest.

Carbon dioxide

Felling and burning rain forests also releases more of a gas called carbon dioxide (CO_2) into the air. CO_2 adds to **climate change**. This destroys many other habitats around the world.

FACT!
- Half of all the species of plants in the world live only in rain forests.
- Every second an area of rain forest the size of two football fields is destroyed.

Many rain forest trees are burned down to clear land for farming.

Western Lowland gorillas are threatened by logging and farming.

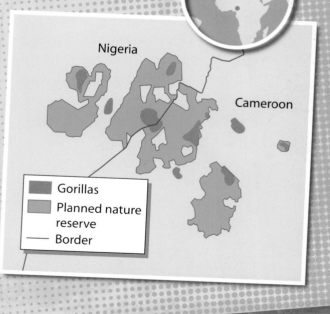

ON THE SPOT
Cameroon

The rain forests of Cameroon are disappearing fast because farmers and logging companies are cutting them down. These rain forests are home to the Western Lowland gorilla. The government of Cameroon wants to save the gorillas. They plan to make a **nature reserve** for them. This means that they will save an area of the rain forest just for the gorillas.

Nigeria

Cameroon

▮ Gorillas
▮ Planned nature reserve
── Border

Logging Threatens the Monarch

LOGGING COMPANIES IN Mexico are threatening a **species** of butterfly called the monarch. Many of these butterflies spend the winter in forests in the mountains of Mexico. Others spend the winter in southern California or Florida. The butterflies spend the summer months in New England and around the Great Lakes.

Butterfly migration

The monarch butterflies start the long journey north in the spring. On the way, they lay eggs that hatch into caterpillars. The butterflies that laid the eggs die, but the caterpillars change into new butterflies. These butterflies continue the journey and lay more eggs. When autumn comes, the surviving butterflies return to their winter homes.

Butterfly reserve

In winter the fir trees in the mountain forests of Mexico become covered with millions of monarch butterflies. They cling to the trunks and branches and **hibernate**. The butterflies fall into a deep sleep until spring. The area is a **nature reserve** for the butterflies. It is called the Biosphere Reserve.

Felling the forest

It is against the law to cut down trees in the reserve, but local people and logging companies continue to do so. More than half of all the trees in the Biosphere Reserve have been cut down already. So many trees have been destroyed that there are fewer places for the butterflies to live. This means there are fewer monarch butterflies.

Caterpillar food

Monarch caterpillars feed only on the nectar of the milkweed flower. These plants are becoming increasingly rare in North America. Farmers are planting **crops** on the land where the milkweed used to grow. This makes it harder for monarch butterflies to survive the journey north in the summer. Some people try to help the monarchs by planting milkweed in their gardens.

BEHIND THE HEADLINES
Milkweed

Milkweed contains a poison that protects monarch caterpillars from **predators**. The poison makes the caterpillar taste bitter. The yellow and black stripes of the caterpillars warn birds to leave them alone. The poison stays in the caterpillar's body as it changes into a butterfly, so monarch butterflies enjoy the same protection, too.

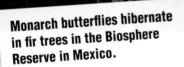

Monarch butterflies hibernate in fir trees in the Biosphere Reserve in Mexico.

A monarch butterfly feeds on the nectar of a milkweed flower.

Pandas Reunited

THERE ARE so few giant pandas living in the wild that they are in danger of becoming **extinct**. **Ecologists** are trying to save the few remaining individuals. They are helping them by linking together the isolated pockets of bamboo forests in which they live.

Isolated groups

In the wild, giant pandas live in the mountains of southwest China, where the waters of the Yangtze River start to flow. The pandas live in the thick bamboo forests, where they feed on juicy bamboo shoots.

However, most of the bamboo forests have been cut down. The wild giant pandas live in the few scattered patches of forest that remain. They live in small groups, making it hard to breed and produce young pandas.

Pandas and people

The area in which the pandas live is important for people, too. They need it for fishing and farming. They use the Yangtze River to generate **hydroelectric power**.

Planting corridors

Is there room for pandas as well as people? One way to help is by planting bamboo corridors between the isolated patches of bamboo forest. These corridors will join the panda groups.

Bamboo is one of the fastest-growing plants. Once the land has been set aside for these corridors, it takes only a few years for the bamboo trees to grow and unite the isolated panda groups.

Giant pandas are fussy eaters. Bamboo shoots are their favorite food.

ON THE SPOT
China

China

Qinling Mountains

People have planted a bamboo "corridor" in China's Qinling Mountains. It joins two panda groups that became separated when a road was built through the forest in 1983. In 1999, a road tunnel was built through the mountain to replace the road. The government made the area into a **nature reserve**. Volunteers planted bamboo along the abandoned road. They have reunited 20 pandas on Mount Tianhuashan with the 110 pandas on Mount Xinglongling. During the 2008 earthquake, many buildings were damaged in the panda reserves, but the forests and pandas survived unharmed.

Bamboo trees form thick forests in some parts of China, but most have been cleared for farming.

Will Cod Make a Comeback?

JUST 50 YEARS ago, cod were common in the Atlantic Ocean. Today, people who fish the waters are only allowed to catch small numbers of cod. This is because there are not many cod left in the Atlantic.

Fishing controls are giving the cod a chance to increase in numbers. If the controls fail, cod may become so expensive that only rich people will be able to afford it. At worst, cod might disappear as a food source completely.

What happened?

In the 1990s, scientists realized that cod were disappearing from the Gulf of St. Lawrence off of Canada. The people who fished these waters were catching so many fish that there were not enough left to produce new fish. This is called **overfishing**. In 1992, Canada **banned** cod fishing.

Rocky road to recovery

People expected the population to increase within a few years in Canada – but it didn't. Around 15 years after the ban, there are only small cod left and too few to start fishing again.

The same thing may happen in European waters, where there are half as many cod as there should be. The European Union stops fishermen from catching too many cod. It hopes that by acting quickly, the cod will recover sooner.

Large cod like this one are now rare because of overfishing.

BEHIND THE HEADLINES
Dolphin friendly

In the Pacific Ocean, schools of yellowfin tuna often swim below dolphins. People who fish for tuna knew that if they caught dolphins in their fishing nets, they would catch the tuna, too. Dolphins die in fishing nets because they cannot come to the surface to breathe. People fishing for tuna can help the dolphins by not using nets. Instead, they can use fishing lines to catch one tuna at a time.

Before people buy canned tuna, they should make sure it is "line caught" or "dolphin friendly."

Great Barrier Reef Turns White

CORAL REEFS ARE usually very colorful, but in April 2002 Australia's world-famous **coral reef**, the Great Barrier Reef, suddenly turned white. This is called **bleaching**.

Bleaching happens when the tiny animals that make up the reef begin to die. If the coral dies, the fish and other creatures that depend on it for food and shelter die, too.

Up to 95 percent of the Great Barrier Reef became bleached in some areas in 2002. However, the bleaching did not affect the entire reef. Only about 10 percent of the coral in the reef died as a result of the 2002 bleaching.

Too warm for comfort

The Great Barrier Reef became bleached in 2002 because a heat wave made the sea much warmer.

Coral reefs are made up of billions of **coral polyps**. These tiny animals provide a home for plants called **algae**. The algae make food that the polyps eat.

The color of the coral comes from the colors of the algae. If the water temperature becomes too warm or too cool, the polyps push the algae out. Then the coral loses its color and its source of food. Without food, the coral begins to die.

Warming oceans

Luckily, after a few weeks, the sea soon cooled down around the Great Barrier Reef and most of the coral recovered. Scientists have found that the world's oceans are steadily becoming warmer. This is because of **global warming**. It means that more coral is likely to become bleached in the future, and it may not recover.

FACT!

✦ The Great Barrier Reef is the world's longest chain of underwater reefs and coral islands.
✦ Unless global warming slows down, almost all of the coral that makes up the Great Barrier Reef could become bleached by 2050.

BEHIND THE HEADLINES
Global warming

The Earth is warming up faster than ever before. This is because people are using more **fossil fuels**. They burn them to make electricity and to use as fuel in vehicles. Burning fossil fuels creates **greenhouse gases**. These gases mix with the air and trap some of the Sun's heat. This warms up the air above the land and the sea.

The Great Barrier Reef lies off the east coast of Australia. More species of sea animals live among coral reefs than anywhere else in the ocean.

This coral reef is in the Caribbean Sea. Much of the coral here is already bleached.

Too Warm for Polar Bears

GLOBAL WARMING is also threatening the lives of polar bears. Polar bears hunt seals around the icy Arctic Ocean. The Arctic Ocean is so cold that some of the seawater freezes and becomes sea ice. Seals live in the ocean on the edge of the sea ice. As the Earth warms up, the ice is melting faster. This gives the polar bears less time to hunt for the seals.

Melting sea ice

In the spring, some of the sea ice along the coast melts and breaks up to form pack ice. This is the best time for polar bears to hunt for seals. In the summer, the sea ice is too far from land for the polar bears to reach it. In the autumn, the sea around the coast begins to refreeze and the polar bears can hunt again. During this short time, the polar bears must eat a lot of seals. They need to put on enough fat to survive the long winter months.

Thin and starving

Today the sea ice is melting earlier in the spring and freezing later in the autumn. This gives the polar bears less time to hunt before winter. Many polar bears are not getting enough food and are thinner than they used to be. In addition, more sea ice melts in the Arctic each year. Scientists predict that by the year 2050 there will be no sea ice at all in the summer. If that happens polar bears will disappear from much of the Arctic.

Polar bears hunt seals that live on the sea ice around the edge of the Arctic Ocean.

ON THE SPOT
Canada

It is autumn in Churchill in northern Canada. The area is packed with tourists. They have come to see the polar bears. The bears gather to wait for the sea ice to form. In the past, people shot the hungry bears because they invaded their kitchens looking for food. Today, the bears are held in a special pen, called the "bear jail," instead.

This hungry polar bear has been attracted to a tourist bus by the smell of food.

Caribou or Oil?

OIL COMPANIES IN Alaska could make life very difficult for the caribou that live there. The companies want to mine **oil** that lies under the **tundra**. The tundra is covered with moss in the summer and ice in the winter. The caribou **migrate** to the tundra in the summer to feed on the moss. **Ecologists** are scientists who study **habitats**. They say that drilling for oil will block the caribou's migration route.

In the summer, caribou graze on the tundra. In the autumn, they travel south to spend the winter in warmer places.

On the move
Alaskan caribou spend the winter in southern Alaska. In the spring, they walk thousands of miles to the tundra. There, the females give birth to young calves. The caribou and calves graze and put on weight to see them through the winter.

Blocking the way
If oil companies are allowed to drill for oil, they will need to build roads and pipelines across the land. These roads and pipelines will stop the caribou from moving freely.

The huge Trans-Alaska pipeline carries oil across Alaska. Ecologists argue that it is already blocking the migration route of the caribou. Building more roads and pipelines will only add to the problem.

Woodland caribou
Woodland caribou live in the forests of Alberta in Canada. These caribou are also threatened by the oil industry. Oil companies are clearing the woodlands and destroying the caribou's habitat. There are now so few woodland caribou left in Alberta that they are in danger of becoming **extinct**.

We need to drill for oil in Alaska: Who is right and who is wrong?

FOR

People need oil to run cars, planes, and other vehicles, and to generate electricity. Oil companies do their best to protect the **territory** of the caribou. In some places, they bury the pipeline. In other places, they provide ramps for the caribou to cross over the pipeline.

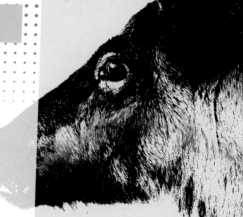

The Trans-Alaska pipeline carries oil across Alaska. It stretches from oil wells in Prudhoe Bay in the north to the port of Valdez in southern Alaska.

AGAINST

Oil is the problem. Burning oil adds to **global warming**. Drilling for oil in Alaska damages caribou habitat. We need to ensure that all cars and planes do not burn **fossil fuels**. There are other ways of generating electricity, such as **hydroelectric power**.

Sea Birds Killed by Plastic Trash

Some sea birds are feeding their chicks plastic trash instead of fish. The birds nest on the islands of the Midway **Atoll** in the middle of the Pacific Ocean. Every day the beaches of these islands are littered with trash, such as bits of plastic and fishing nets. The birds think the plastic is fish.

Where does all the trash come from?

The people who live on Midway do not dump the plastic into the sea. Only 30 people live on the islands, and most of them are there to protect the sea birds. Most of the trash is thrown into the sea by people in North America and Southeast Asia. Some of it is thrown in by sailors on ships. Plastic does not rot. The ocean carries the trash thousands of miles before it washes up on the shores of Midway and other Hawaiian islands.

Plastic problems

Scientists have examined many birds on Midway. In one study, scientists found that nine out of ten chicks had plastic trash in their stomachs. The people who live on Midway regularly clear the beaches, but they cannot collect all the trash from the sea. As a result, the plastic problem is getting much worse.

Too heavy to fly

Some young birds eat so much plastic that they become too heavy to fly. As a result, they cannot hunt for food or meet a mate. The young birds will not survive as adults.

Around one-third of albatross chicks die before they become adults. Some chicks choke to death on the plastic trash. Other chicks starve because their stomachs are full of plastic, and there is not enough room for real food.

FACT!

- ✦ Dolphins and seals become entangled in abandoned plastic fishing nets and drown.
- ✦ Plastic trash breaks up into small, poisonous beads that have been found inside many fish.

ON THE SPOT
Midway

Midway is a coral atoll in the middle of the Pacific Ocean. It is farther north than any other Hawaiian island. Midway is a **nature reserve** for sea birds.

This amount of plastic trash washed up on the beach in just one day. To stop this happening, people need to make sure that no trash reaches the sea.

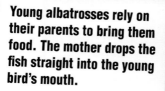

Young albatrosses rely on their parents to bring them food. The mother drops the fish straight into the young bird's mouth.

Hunted Almost to Extinction

POACHERS ARE PEOPLE who hunt animals illegally. For example, it is against the law to hunt black rhinos in Africa and Sumatran tigers from Indonesia. **Poachers** kill them anyway.

Poachers have already wiped out one kind of rhino and four kinds of tiger. Unless the poachers are stopped, the remaining rhinos and tigers could become **extinct**.

Black rhinos

Black rhinos are hunted for their horns. For hundreds of years the horns have been made into decorated dagger handles. The horn is also powdered and used in **traditional remedies**. There is no evidence that these drugs work. However, poachers still make a lot of money from the rhino horn.

Today, almost all black rhinos live in **national parks** and reserves.

Game wardens work very hard to protect them from the poachers.

Sumatran tigers

The Sumatran tiger is the only **species** of tiger that still survives in Indonesia. There are between 400 and 500 Sumatran tigers still living in the wild. However, poachers are killing these rare tigers and selling their skin, teeth, and claws to traders. The teeth and claws are used in traditional remedies and sold to people in Cambodia, Indonesia, Myanmar, and many other countries in Southeast Asia.

Stopping the poachers

Animal **charities** are trying to persuade the Indonesian government to set some of their land aside to make **nature reserves**. The tigers would enjoy some protection from the poachers. Only then would the numbers of tigers start to increase.

FACT!
- A hundred years ago, 100,000 tigers lived in the wild.
- Today, around 3,000 tigers are known to still live as wild animals.

Black rhinos live in eastern and central parts of Africa.

ON THE SPOT
Indonesia

In August 2004, five men in Indonesia were found guilty of poaching tigers. They were sent to prison for six years. The men had poisoned the tigers and sold them to a network of traders. The traders had paid poachers for at least 60 tigers in the last ten years. Local police and game wardens say that the prison sentence is helping to stop other poachers.

Poachers are killing tigers for their skins, which fetch a high price at market.

Activists Fight Back

In December 2007, **animal-rights activists** chased a fleet of Japanese whaling ships through the Southern Ocean. The whaling fleet wanted to kill 935 minke whales and 50 fin whales. Whales are killed with long spears called **harpoons**. International laws allow them to do this, because Japan claimed that the whales were for scientific study. The activists wanted to save the whales from being killed.

The chase

Animal-rights activists chased the whaling ships in two small boats. They planned to save the whales by sailing between them and the whaling ships. Instead of hunting whales, the whaling ships sailed around in circles. After several weeks, the activists' boats ran out of fuel.

They were forced to return to port. The whaling ships then hunted the whales. However, the activists had delayed the whaling ships and may have saved the lives of hundreds of whales.

Humpback whales

In the past, so many humpback whales were hunted that they almost became **extinct**. Hunting all whales was **banned**. However, laws allowed a few whales to be killed for scientific study. The number of whales gradually began to increase. In 2006, Japan said that they were going to kill 50 humpback whales in 2007. **Ecologists** around the world were outraged. In December 2007, the Japanese changed their minds. This was a victory for the animal-rights activists.

Whaling was once so widespread that some **species** of whale almost died out.

Whaling is necessary:
Who is right and who is wrong?

FOR

Hunting supporter: We believe there are now plenty of whales. We only kill a few so that we can study them.

Australian anti-whaling activists clash with a Japanese whaling ship in December 2007.

AGAINST

Animal-rights activist: Hunting these highly intelligent creatures is cruel and unnecessary. You can gather information without killing the whales.

Intensive Farming Hurts Chickens

MOST FARM ANIMALS are not in danger of **extinction**, but some are kept in such cruel conditions that their lives are not worth living.

Forced to feed

Broiler chickens are hens that grow faster than normal chickens. They are fed with special feed and drugs, which make them grow even faster. This type of farming is called **intensive farming**, and it produces cheap meat.

These chickens are being intensively farmed. The cages are so small that they cannot move.

Cramped conditions

Some farmers keep their chickens in crowded cages and sheds. Sometimes the conditions are so cramped that the chickens cannot move. Some of them have been fed so much food that they are too heavy to move. Their legs cannot support their own weight. The floor is deep in droppings. The droppings infect open sores on the hens' legs and chests. The chickens can become ill and die.

A natural life

Animal-rights activists think that people should stop buying chicken produced by intensive farming. There is an alternative.

Some farmers allow their chickens to live in a natural way. The chickens can walk around outside and explore, just like the wild relatives of chickens do. They are fed on grass or corn and grow more slowly. This is called **free-range** farming. It costs more to farm chickens in this way, and so their meat is more expensive.

Intensive farming is good:
Who is right and who is wrong?

FOR

Intensive farming produces huge amounts of cheap food. We need cheap food to feed the world. The birds are not allowed to move so that all their energy goes into making more meat. Free-range farming will never produce as much meat.

AGAINST

We don't have the right to treat animals in this way to produce cheap meat. If farm animals had the same rights as pets, intensive farmers would be put in prison. Many people eat too much meat. They would be healthier if they ate less.

Free-range chickens are allowed to go outside. These birds have strong legs. They are a different shape than chickens that have been farmed intensively.

Get Involved!

EVERYONE CAN HELP to save animals under threat. One way to get involved is to find out what animal **charities** do and how you can support them. You can encourage your family and friends to take action, too.

Wildlife charities

There are many different wildlife charities. Some **campaign** on behalf of many different animals. For example, the World Wildlife Fund campaigns for many animals that are threatened with **extinction**. Other charities campaign for just one **species**.

For example, Pandas International are devoted to protecting giant pandas and their **habitats**.

What do they do?

Some charities set up animal hospitals. They buy medical supplies and hire veterinary surgeons to treat injured wild animals. Other charities buy land and build **nature reserves** to protect particular animals. They may try to persuade governments to pass laws to help animals. For example, they might campaign for laws that make selling rhino horns illegal.

Wildlife charities are helping to protect giant pandas by preserving their natural habitat.

THINGS TO DO

Shopping

- Check that canned tuna is "dolphin friendly" or "line-caught."
- Buy **free-range** products.
- Do not buy anything made of wood from **rain forests**, such as mahogany or teak.
- On vacation, do not buy items made from **ivory** (elephant tusks), rhino horn, or coral.

Balloons can drift out to sea, where animals might swallow and choke on them.

Litter

- Do not drop litter, especially plastic, in the street. Litter that gets washed from the street into drains can end up in the ocean.
- Do not let balloons float off into the air. When they fall back down, they are often washed into the sea. There they may kill sea animals that eat them.

Gardens

- Find out what you can plant in your garden to provide food for insects and birds.

Save energy

- Avoid using cars and planes as much as you can to slow down **global warming**.
- Switch off lights and don't waste electricity, so that less **fossil fuel** is burned in power stations.

Charities

- Charities sometimes run online petition campaigns that you can join.
- You can support a charity by arranging events, such as bake sales, to raise money.

Glossary

alga (more than one: **algae**) tiny plant-like organism that makes its own food

animal-rights activist person who campaigns on behalf of animals

atoll ring-shaped coral reef that surrounds a lagoon

banned not allowed to do something

bleaching when something loses its color and becomes white

campaign to speak for and work on behalf of

charity organization that collects money and uses it to help good causes

climate change unexpected changes to the weather caused by global warming

coral polyp tiny animal that lives in warm oceans

coral reef long ridge of coral made when coral polyps build their shells on the top of old shells

crop plant grown by farmers

ecologist scientist who studies living things in their habitat

extinct when no member of a species still exists in nature

fossil fuel fuel such as oil and gas that formed from the remains of plants and animals that lived millions of years ago

free-range when farm animals are allowed to wander outside

global warming increase in the average temperature at the surface of the Earth

greenhouse gas gas that traps the Sun's heat and leads to global warming

habitat place where animals and plants normally live in the wild

harpoon spear attached to a rope

hibernate deep sleep that some animals fall into to survive the cold winter

hydroelectric power electricity that is generated by the force of running water

intensive farming farming in which animals are kept in crowded conditions and given special food and/or drugs to make them more productive

ivory material that is obtained from the tusks of elephants

logging cutting down trees to sell the wood for timber

migrate to move from one place to another. Some animals migrate to find food at certain times of the year.

national park area of land put aside by governments to protect living things

nature reserve area of land managed by people to protect wildlife

oil liquid that forms under the ground and is burned as a fuel

overfishing when people catch more of one kind of fish than are being replaced by young fish

poacher person who breaks the law by hunting animals

predator animal that hunts other animals for food

rain forest thick forest where it rains heavily almost every day

scrubland land where only small bushes grow because the soil is dry and poor

species particular kind of living thing

territory particular area of land where an animal lives and hunts

traditional remedy medicine that has been made by people for hundreds of years and sometimes includes animal parts

tundra swampy land around the Arctic Ocean that is frozen in winter

Find Out More

Books

Allen, Julia and Margaret Iggulden. *Animal Rights (Your Environment)*. Mankato, MN: Stargazer Books, 2007.

Bellamy, Rufus. *Saving Wildlife (Action for the Environment)*. Mankato, MN: Black Rabbit Books, 2005.

Goldish, Meish. *Red Wolves: And Then There Were Almost None (America's Animal Comebacks)*. New York: Bearport Publishing, 2009.

Green, Jen. *Wildlife in Danger (Your Environment)*. Mankato, MN: Stargazer Books, 2005.

Pobst, Sandy. *Animals on the Edge: Science Races to Save Species Threatened with Extinction (National Geographic Investigates)*. Washington, DC: National Geographic Society, 2008.

Websites

This site is all about the rain forest and some of the animals that live there, including gorillas:
http://kids.mongabay.com/

Pandas International is a charity that works to save pandas. The Caring Kids section gives many ideas for things you can do:
www.pandasinternational.org

Save the Whales is a charity that works to protect whales from hunting. Their website gives information about campaigns and how you can help to save the whales:
www.savethewhales.org/about.html

This is the student center website of the United States Environmental Protection Agency (EPA). It includes projects, activities, and other information about the environment and how it can be conserved:
www.epa.gov/students/

Index